People are meowin
and *The Wisdon*

CW00738612

"*The Wisdom of a Psychic Cat* is an absolutely delightful book that is fun to read and filled with lots of inspirational ideas for living a happier life. It will make a great gift for the cat lovers in your life and for anyone else looking for guidance on practical ways to increase the happiness in their lives." ~ Laurence Andrews, author of *Secrets of the Silk Road - Finding the Lost Sacred Books of the Gobi*

"Although it is humbling to gain wisdom from a cat, sometimes if we separate ourselves from the human experience, the truth of our existence rises to the surface. In this whimsical story, the reader becomes a student learning how to shed the layers of domestication and reveal the "wilderness underneath." ~ William Buhlman, author of *Adventures Beyond the Body* and *Adventures in the Afterlife*

"This creative book by Jessica McKay is like catnip for your soul. Easy to read and entertaining, *The Wisdom of a Psychic Cat* opens your heart. Even if you are allergic to cats, you will find the fifteen lessons practical and powerful wisdom." ~ Regina Cates, author of *Lead With Your Heart, Creating a Life of Love, Compassion and Purpose.*

"I have enjoyed many cats in my life, but never one as wise as this psychic cat! She shares astounding insights and important teachings for we humans. Thank you, Jessica, for collecting this wisdom." ~ Allan Hardman, author of *The Everything Toltec Wisdom Book*

"A rich collection of insights from one very wise soul. This cat has been places and seen things that will lift your spirits and enlighten your mind. This is a beautiful book!" ~ Melissa Phillippe and Z Egloff, authors of *Everyday Joy - 365 Days of OhMyGod Life*

"In this absolutely delightful and imaginative book, Jessica McKay applies her strong, admirable writing talents to an exploration of the human world viewed through the mind and consciousness of a very evolved, very wise cat named "Little Girlie." If you have ever wondered what your cat is "thinking," you will find this book both entertaining and enlightening. It is enormously accessible... easy to read, yet offering an abundance of valuable spiritual insight. You will find yourself enthralled by Little Girlie's reflections on the confusions and perplexities of human values, and the bizarre behavior she observes in the human world around her. This is a book that is both "fun," AND provocative... offering layer upon layer of truly fascinating opportunities to see life differently... through the eyes and the mind of a cat." ~ Ramananda John E. Welshons, author of *One Soul, One Love, One Heart* and *Awakening from Grief*

The Wisdom of
a Psychic Cat

The Wisdom of a Psychic Cat

15 Lessons on Happiness for Humans

Jessica McKay

*The Wisdom of a Psychic Cat ~ 15 Lessons on
Happiness for Humans*

Cover design: Raess Design
Sketch Art: Ermir Kolonja
("Videosketch" on Fiverr.com)

ISBN 10 1717363652
ISBN 13 978-1717363657

Dedicated to the memory of Buddy Hardman

I hear rustling.
Basement mouse invites kill-bite.
Cat food, you grow cold.

~ Little Girlie McFluff, Psychic Cat Oracle and
Great Wild One

ACKNOWLEDGMENTS

I'd like to thank the spiritual teachers who inspired my creative journey and whose teaching made this book come alive: William Buhlman, Allan Hardman, Francis Rico Hayhurst and Neale Donald Walsch.

I'd also like to thank Marian R. Stuart, Ph.D. for the perspective on forgiveness which inspired chapter 14, and Ramananda John E. Welshons for helping me hone my message.

I'm so grateful for my talented editing team: Tamara Protassow and Wendy Warren Varga. Mom, your creativity and attention to detail made this book even better than I imagined. Thank you!

I'd also like to thank Ted and Peggy Raess of Raess Design, who created the beautiful cover.

Colin, thank you for teaching me, through your patience and love, how to be a proper servant-guardian to a cat.

And finally, I *must* thank Little Girlie McFluff, my friend and muse, for allowing me to bask in her enlightened presence.

CONTENTS

Foreword   i

Introduction   1

Lesson 1: Be Yourself   5

Lesson 2: Practice Gratitude   10

Lesson 3: Know that You are Lovable   15

Lesson 4: Be Open to Adventure   19

Lesson 5: Embrace the Silence   24

Lesson 6: Silence Your Tyrants   27

Lesson 7: Practice Self-Acceptance   31

Lesson 8: Become Aware of Your Power to   36
Choose

Lesson 9: Surrender and Let Go   41

Lesson 10: Change Your Perception of Time   44
and Space

Lesson 11: Allow Yourself to Play   54

Lesson 12: Learn the Art of Selfishness   61

Lesson 13: Tell Yourself a New Story   66

Lesson 14: Learn the True Art of Forgiveness   72

Lesson 15: Remember Who You Really Are   79

A Love Note   84

PREPARING TO LEAP FORWARD

Foreword by Maria "Meme" Fernandez-O'Neill

My name is Meme. I am presently embodied as a remarkably beautiful Tortoiseshell cat. Until this lifetime, I exclusively incarnated as a jaguar – living in many jungles, in many jaguaresque variations – but always as a stealthy and elegant creature of light and shadow.

I was called into the world of humans by the cry for help from the wild creatures of this world, and I recognize a kindred spirit in Little Girlie. However, she is responding directly to the cry of alarm and desperation that is coming *from* the humans – *they* are her concern!

What has happened to humans? What is the source of so much distress? Not only the distress that humans experience, but also the awful distress that humans inflict on others?

Personally, I've always tried to steer clear of humans — until now. Instead of a jaguar, I decided to incarnate as a cat and involve myself with a couple — a shaman and an artist — considering them to be a bridge into understanding what the problem is here on our planet.

On the other paw, Little Girlie chose to dive directly into the heart of the matter: her concern is for *you* – and she reveals the wisdom that comes from having lived over 500 lifetimes as a human being before she chose to incarnate as a cat. She offers a series of lessons that are clear, direct, and essential to happiness and wholeness.

Please listen to Little Girlie! My prayer for you who read her words: may you find happiness. And, to the precious and brave wild heart that brings herself here to heal and help humankind: *Thank you, Little Girlie!*

~ Maria "Meme" Fernandez - O'Neill
(and Francis Rico Hayhurst)

INTRODUCTION

My name in this lifetime is Little Girlie. My surname, McFluff, was given to me by my servant-guardian, Jessica, and I had no objections to accepting it.

I'm a psychic cat. I make predictions about the changing of the seasons, have access to my past lives, and communicate telepathically with those who can hear me. I came to live with Jessica by sending a signal, in the form of a telepathic impulse, to the woman working at the Humane Society where I was adopted. She obeyed my mental nudging when Jessica arrived desiring "an affectionate cat." In other words, she wanted to be able to pick me up and hold me like a baby. I hate being picked up but pretended to enjoy it during her visit. I agreed to go home with her because I felt intuitively that she was also psychic — so there was a good chance she'd be capable of hearing my telepathic messages.

The first time we spoke, she was quite surprised to learn that this is my 313th life as a cat, and before this, I lived over 500 lifetimes as a human being. That is why I understand human nature so well, and why I'm qualified to expound upon happiness as it relates to humans. As befitting a proper servant-guardian, Jessica vowed to write down my stories and bring my wisdom into the world.

I have remembered much from various incarnations — cat *and* human. You might wonder why I made the epic transition from human to animal, and more particularly, cat. To me, the answer is obvious, but you probably haven't experienced the superior consciousness that comes with being a feline — so I'll break down my experience for you.

Animal friends who revere me as "The Great Wild One" are always asking if it's really true that I used to be human — as so few of them would ever consider incarnating as one. Indeed, it is true, and I was remembering some of these lifetimes during my nap. In one of them I was a warrior who killed many. In another, I was a young girl who died of starvation. In another, a mother with nine children.

I desired a break from humanity after a while, and the next time around decided to be a bird. After that, I chose walrus, hippo, and wildebeest. I was zebra and monkey. And finally, I decided to experience the consciousness of Cat. I have found that nothing is better than cat, and truly, I cannot imagine coming to Earth as anything else.

Some of my cat lives were difficult. I caught mice in a barn in the 1700's and was homeless in the streets of London in the 1830's. But overall, it's been a blissful existence.

In this form, I am allowed to act out my nature. Nobody scolds me for doing what comes naturally. My impulse to kill is celebrated instead of shamed. I can be demanding about getting my needs met without anyone telling me I'm selfish. My long naps are regarded as appropriate cat behavior rather than laziness, and my routine never gets old. With a cat's awareness, life is never boring. I live and breathe, I chase and kill, I luxuriate in my meals, and I love others the way only a cat can love: unconditionally, candidly, and innocently. Never am I jaded or jealous.

But do not despair, my human friend! Your mind is so creative that you can easily imagine what it's like to be a cat:

- Pretend that you have permission to be yourself, totally.
- Pretend that none of your urges are wrong.
- Pretend that none of your desires are wrong, and none of your feelings are wrong. They are just right for you. They are perfect!

The more you pretend, the more real it will seem, until you realize that it *is* real and you are free of human guilt and shame. On a sad day, perhaps long ago, somebody criticized you for being flawed and you believed that criticism. It's time to wake up from that dream and claim your freedom with me. Tune into my vibration, my wild cat energy. Tune into my joy and the bliss of my life. They are here for you, and you'll recognize them because they are within you.

In this book, I share 15 lessons intended to inspire happiness in humans — something I struggled very hard to achieve myself as a human being. When I became a cat, I discovered that napping goes a long way, and it is often overlooked as a powerful spiritual tool. What follows are stories, lessons, and advice so deep you may have to rest after reading them.

~ Little Girlie McFluff, Psychic Cat Oracle and Great Wild One

4

LESSON 1:
BE YOURSELF

Who are you?

You, my wild friend, are a miracle. You are an individual expression of Divinity, but you have forgotten. How do I know this? *Please...* I'm a cat. I know much more than you can ever imagine. Plus, I have the benefit of remembering my many trips around the circle of life and death. But between us there are similarities. Like me, you were born with a very unique set of preferences. When you were a baby, nobody had to tell you whether you liked something — you just knew. And when you need-ed something, there was no confusion about that, either. Before you knew language, you had the lan-guage of your emotions which burst forth to inform you — and your parents — that you had needs.

Emotions were the only form of communication and information you had.

As you matured to interpret signals from your parents, you began learning that this wellspring of information was not always welcome. Your parents began downloading their version of what was right or wrong with you into your mind. You learned their beliefs about good and bad behavior, and may have been told to go to your room and not come out until you could stop crying and having emotional reactions.

If this happened to you, it may have been shocking to learn that the truth bubbling up from your belly was somehow wrong and not welcome. I know what this feels like because I was domesticated by over 500 sets of human parents. In almost every one of these lifetimes I was shamed for emotions like fear and anger, and learned to hide them well. Just as you may have been taught that you weren't okay exactly the way you were, I was taught that I was flawed. I spent the first few years of each human lifetime learning how my tribe and family wanted me to behave so I could be worthy of their acceptance and love. Through 500 lifetimes I carried the immense burden of my domestication, and I domesticated my own children in the same way.

As humans, you've forgotten your Divinity. You've been passing down a perception of imperfection and unworthiness, and believing it. You've forgotten that your nature is love. You *are* love, and as a baby, you were in touch with the pure, unconditional acceptance of self. You didn't judge anything. You may have felt the discomfort that comes with being in a human body, but you had no opinions or stories attached to it. On some level, even if you can't remember now, you *knew* that you were wonderful, lovable, and just right the way you were. This knowingness came to an abrupt halt when, perhaps for the first time, you were made wrong for expressing some aspect of yourself. The beginning of your domestication began the process of forgetting who you really are — and your happiness depends on remembering!

You are a unique manifestation of creation, born with your own special combination of likes, dislikes and preferences because you were meant to come here as *you*, not someone else. Indeed, you are the only version of you that has ever existed, and the only version that will ever exist in the entire span of the universe. You deserve to embrace your uniqueness and celebrate it. But humans are so busy trying to please others that their uniqueness gets lost in their struggle to be worthy of love.

I, on the other hand, am completely undomesticated. You can't hold my attention long enough to teach me your version of right or wrong, and my superior cat brain doesn't register punishment. There's a tremendous amount of freedom in that, because you can't tell me who I'm supposed to be and what I'm supposed to do to earn your approval and love.

You can only be you, and I can only be me. Jessica can talk all she wants about her previous cat, Buddy, who put up with being carried like a baby — and it's not going to have any effect on me. I *despise* being carried, and she loves me anyway. She loves me even though I have a bald spot on my coat, drool when I'm being combed, and claim the best spot on the couch. She continues to love me even though I have shown a marked preference for the attentions given to me by her husband. He knows the very instant I have a need and jumps up to attend me. At first Jessica was outraged and banished him from feeding me in the hopes that I would like her best, but the strategy had no effect. She fed me and I still preferred his company. I do not feel guilty or ashamed about these preferences that arise naturally from within.

Over time, Jessica learned how to respect my preferences by accepting me unconditionally, and that is when my relationship with her deepened. I really gave her no choice in the matter.

If you want to be happy, you need to know that you are lovable just the way you are. If you love and accept yourself, it won't matter whether others approve. But I'm psychic and I know what you're thinking. You're thinking, "Little Girlie, you're just an animal. People accept you and let you do what you want because you are not human. Nobody can train you not to take the best spot on the couch. You can't be domesticated!"

Here's what I say to that: you're an animal too. Yes, you are wild! And while you might be trainable like my subservient dog friends, I know you can hearken back to the wildness underneath the civilized behaviors you were taught. You can consciously accept yourself the way you are, and tell the people domesticating you that you're too wild to heed their tiresome words. That's what I do. I walk out of the room. I turn my back. I'm a master of wildness and joyfully surrender to it.

Why should you fight so hard to be different than you are? Why should you fight to be enough? Don't you see, my wild friend, that we are all enough? We have all been created by the same Wild Heart.

LESSON 2:
PRACTICE GRATITUDE

I want to take a blissful moment out of my busy sleeping and eating schedule to tell you about the abundance in my life. Right now, I'm lying on special bedding next to the heat vent on the floor and couldn't be more content. When I was six weeks old and living behind a garage with my siblings, I had no idea how things were going to turn out, but now here I am, belly-up, basking in paradise.

So many of you are concerned about a lack of abundance. You forget that when you were a baby, life took care of you. You were fed, clothed, and had enough, somehow, to make it to this moment. You didn't have to know a thing — you just had to exist. Life also took care of growing your hair, monitoring your heartbeat, and digesting your food.

And now, there are a million things to be grateful for. If you want to be as happy as I am, begin by seeing the small things around you to get excited about. And really, the small things aren't so insignificant. Wars were once fought over coffee, and now it's everywhere. (I know this because of a harrowing journey across the sea with a coffee plant in a previous life. Now I don't see what the big fuss was about — war over a can of tuna fish I would understand, but coffee? Revolting!)

There are humans on this planet who may never know what it's like to have clean water or electricity. If you are reading these words, it's quite possible you are among the wealthiest humans alive right now. I know that Life is taking good care of you. How do I know this? Because no matter how hard your life has been, you are here, reading my words.

When I was a cat in 19th century London, my cousin Bob used to lament that we were alley cats and didn't have warm comfortable homes to live in. I had never lived in a human home as a cat before and professed that I didn't know what I was missing. He told me he saw his aunt Patricia get adopted into one of these homes, and he occasionally caught glimpses of her indoors, her white fluffy coat shiny and lustrous from the attentions of the mistress of the house. He envied her terribly.

I explained to Bob that life was taking care of us, even out in the alley. We lived off plenty of mice and scraps. Bob forgot about Patricia after a few days and we got on with our lives, which is appropriate considering it's only humans that compare themselves to others and wish their lives could be different.

However, it was a human life that really taught me about gratitude. In one of my past lives, I was a young girl named Ella. My mother lived on the outskirts of a village and we were poor. Sometimes we had nothing to eat, as we were forbidden to hunt on the lands where we lived. We were allowed to gather only a tiny amount of firewood, and my brother was beaten one day by the landowner's men for taking wood that had fallen on the forest floor. We were really supposed to take the greener wood still on the trees because it wasn't as convenient as gathering it from the ground. Only the landowner enjoyed that privilege.

It wasn't an easy life, but my mother made us tell her what we were grateful for before we went to bed at night. We would have to name at least three things that gave us joy. The funny thing was, we always came up with more, and eventually she'd tell us to be quiet so she could sleep. We had a hard time not finding things. I was grateful for the long grasses I found that hid me when I wanted time to myself. I was grateful for medicinal herbs that I found on my walks, and I was grateful for my mother, who was positive and brave. My father was gone and many of my siblings had died, but I was grateful that what remained of our family were together. My brother and I would make up songs and sing them during chores, so I was grateful for music. I also loved finding grasshoppers and eating them. And I still love eating grasshoppers! Every time I chomp down on a grasshopper that's made a misguided journey into the basement, I am reminded of my life as Ella.

Because I'm a psychic cat, I am aware that you have more resources than I did in that lifetime. I want you to make a gratitude list and put those small things on it that you may have forgotten: warm blankets, comfortable slippers, a hot cup of tea. Keep going… I'll be right here.

At the Heat Vent

LESSON 3:
KNOW THAT YOU ARE LOVABLE

Do you realize how magnificent I am? Do you grasp the magnitude of my absolute perfection? Bask in it, dear human friend.

You, too, are magnificent. It is not conceited or boastful to admit it. How amazing that you're here! You are a perfect creation of the Divine, and nothing you have ever done is wrong or a mistake. You are so precious and lovable, it's hard to look at you without purring madly! You are a perfectly placed work of art. But many humans worry that their challenges in life are a punishment for something they've done wrong. When I was a human, I felt this way all the time.

In one of my human lifetimes, I was a merchant living in Pompeii when a nearby volcano erupted, unleashing a deadly storm that got worse as the hours went by. I spent my last day in that form praying for God's forgiveness — for what, I did not know, but I knew that if God loved me, He would not allow me to die this way.

The men, women and children who sought shelter with me on the ground floor of a villa assumed our city was being punished, and in our shared terror, we made up all kinds of reasons why such a powerful storm of stones and ash were raining down on our homes and collapsing our roofs.

Suddenly, in the early morning hours, an incredible thing happened. I died, and quickly realized how loved I was. My spirit guides told me none of us were being punished. In fact, they told me the only one able to punish me was myself.

They gave me a similar message after a lifetime in which I was gored by a wild pig. My last thought upon surrendering into unconsciousness was, "If only I wasn't such a selfish person, this wouldn't be happening to me." And again, I woke up to find that I'd died, and my spirit guides showed me that my death had nothing to do with me being selfish. Indeed, they laughed, and said I had been quite oafish, stumbling onto the boar without knowing she was there. That, they said, was one of the reasons I died that day.

My beloved human friend, you may be clumsy in your human form, but you are so precious and so dear. Spirit would never punish you for any reason. You are so loved, so adored, and so needed.

If you've been experiencing relationship challenges, health challenges, or any kind of human difficulty, please know that it is not a punishment for something you've done wrong. Sometimes it's an act of weather, and sometimes it's being in the wrong place at the wrong time. But your soul is not fazed or frightened. Your soul embraces all of these experiences, and truly, you never leave or let go of your physical form before you are ready.

The week before the eruption in Pompeii, I had been thinking about all the things I wanted to experience and would never get a chance to do before I died. I was elderly, and regretting not pursuing a different path. Little did I know, these yearnings were arising in me because my soul was getting ready to depart from that form and move on to something else.

During the lifetime in which I surprised the wild pig, I was in an unhappy marriage — and in that century, divorce was not an option. So I

wandered out into the woods wishing for death...
subconsciously, that is.

Never was I punished. I was just loved. When times are tough and your catnip is stale, rest assured that nobody is judging you and doling out punishment. You are loved and as precious as can be.

Please do something to love and nurture yourself today. It can be giving yourself a gift, time alone, or maybe it's setting a boundary and saying no to someone or something. Maybe it's saying *yes* to something. Maybe it's looking in the mirror and seeing your beauty. As you're loving yourself, I'll be demanding my meals and expressing myself fully.

LESSON 4:
BE OPEN TO ADVENTURE

You may not see life exactly the way I see it, but that doesn't make my perception of the universe less real. Right now, you are watching your life unfold in a way that no one else can see. You are the author of your life, and yet, sometimes you feel out of control.

Even I have these moments. I will refer to one of them as *The Great Lampshade Incident of 2015.* I was having a VERY bad day.

But today is completely new. I never assume that this minute is going to be like the last. I really have no idea what to expect, and that keeps things fresh. Each morning, I awaken at the sound of the first bird, and as I race to the window to see which squirrels and birds are awake, it's truly a day like

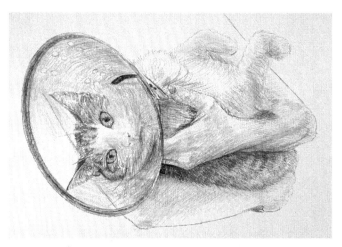

The Great Lampshade Incident of 2015

no other. Yesterday is gone and the future doesn't exist. I've forgotten about the lampshade incident, as well as the mouse that escaped in the dim dark of the basement.

Now I have an empty belly and I'm clamoring for breakfast. I eat!

Now I'm clamoring for Second Breakfast, Elevenses, and Lunch. I eat!

Now I'm being guided to nap in front of the heat vent. I sleep!

Each moment is new for me. Of course, I understand that it's difficult for humans to experience their moments as an unfurling, glorious river of newness. That's why I'm here: to explain how it can work as you move forward in your life.

Many times, you have goals you want to achieve. For example, you say, "I am going to lose weight, beginning now!" And you go on a diet. (Let me just say that I'm quite perplexed by the current human obsession with losing weight. In all my previous lifetimes, cat *and* human, I had to work hard to stay fed. My goal in every life has been to get fat and stay fat. That goes for this lifetime, too, but my servant-guardians don't keep my bowl filled at all times. I must admit, this is a mystery that even my superior cat brain does not comprehend.) Two days into your diet, you get invited to a party and have an extra serving of chicken-flavored hairball treats. You judge yourself because your original intention has drifted and you feel your goal floating away from you.

What you must recognize is that you are not the consistent, plodding, rational creature you imagine yourself to be. You are actually a wild and unpredictable being at heart. You zigzag around on the currents of ever-changing desires and emotions. Thus, it might feel important to lose weight right now, but in a month, you might have a deeper desire driving you.

This is okay. Do you know how many times I've been headed for my food bowl, only to get distracted by movement under the curtains? Investigating my surroundings is a rich experience I wouldn't have if I wasn't a wild creature.

Just the other day, I was settling down for my afternoon nap when I heard Jessica scream. My ears flew back and my eyes darted. My instinct was to run in the opposite direction, and I took off like a wildebeest being pursued by a lion, my nails skidding on the wood floor as I ran. But just as I reached the basement door, Jessica's husband Colin swept me into his arms and ran toward the terrible noise, with me jostling up and down clumsily in his grasp. Colin set me down where Jessica was pointing and yelling. I saw nothing, but heard it immediately: a mouse!

I wanted Jessica and Colin to go away so I could hunt in peace, but they stood around waving and shouting. They moved the furniture, uncovered the mouse's hiding spot, and it ran under the couch. Jessica screamed again, but this time her scream faded into the background as I stalked my prey. I eventually tired the mouse so much that Colin captured it and took it outside, which I thought completely unnecessary. I would have loved to take it down to the basement, bat it around for a while, and then hide it in a place that only I knew. But sometimes I don't get my way in the world of the servant-guardians.

Now, when I hear Jessica scream, I still run in the opposite direction because running away from noise is in my blood. But when you live as though every day is new, and you do not make assumptions that everything is going to be the same, you open your mind to new possibilities. Aim for something you want, and then enjoy where your wildness takes you. Direct your boat, then let go of the oars and go on an adventure.

LESSON 5:
EMBRACE THE SILENCE

In our current technological age, your species has become quite sedentary — and when one aspect of yourself is under-utilized, another must compensate. As your bodies have become less active, your minds have become very bossy and very big. Indeed, I do not know how your brain fits within the confines of your skull.

Of course, the nature of the human mind has always been chaotic. Of the 500 human lifetimes I experienced, I enjoyed a quiet mind in just two of them. In one, I was a Tibetan monk, and in the other, I drew cave art with my Aboriginal tribe in what is now called Australia.

My cat mind is intensely quiet. I do not project myself into the future or think about the past. As a result, my power of focus is unrivaled. When I demand my meals, nothing will deter me. Any attempt to distract me from my purpose is thwarted as I remain fixated on my bowl.

Since you are not a cat and have a noisier mind, a very effective tool to develop your power of focus is meditation. Many humans complain that meditation is almost impossible. They say they cannot possibly quiet their minds. Let me explain what meditation really is. Meditation is *noticing* your thoughts, not quieting them. There is a difference.

Having lived as a human, I am well aware that human thoughts are not very interesting. Indeed, why would you even want to notice them? The magic of noticing your thoughts creates precious space between you and your babbling mind. You become aware that you are *not* your thoughts and *not* your mind. You realize that you are the silent witness, hearing the discord of mental noise as it flows by like a muddy river.

One element that will assist you in meditation is peace and quiet. It is not easy to find quiet on this planet anymore, but I request that you try. In every lifetime I have been a cat, I've had to contend with the noise of humans. Cats have an elevated sense of hearing, so the sounds that seem insignificant to you are approximately five times louder to me. Airplanes, garbage trucks, lawn mowers, leaf blowers, construction workers with pic axes and jackhammers, trucks backing up, televisions, phones and fireworks add to what was already a cacophony of human noise in previous centuries.

Dear one, be still, be silent, tread softly, allow yourself to hear the sounds of nature as they cut through humanity's din. Stop to feel your heartbeat every now and then. Sit in the quiet so you may observe your thoughts and remember, you are the silence under the sound, and in that silence, I exist as well. Let us enter that silence together now, shall we?

LESSON 6:
SILENCE YOUR TYRANTS

Do you have tyrants in your life? I do. My servant-guardians are tyrants. They boss me from one room to the next. I'm manhandled and bullied and squeezed. I hardly get any rest outside my 16+ hours of sleep per day.

"When are you going to catch the cricket in the basement?" they shout.

"Here, chase this ball and get some exercise!"

"Come over here so we can clip your nails."

"Come over here so we can clean your teeth."

"Take your hairball medicine."

I try to transmit messages telepathically — messages like, "Let me choke on this hairball in peace." I know Jessica hears me. For some mysterious reason she chooses not to heed my instructions.

Today I want to warn you about the most dangerous tyrant of all. It's the tyrant who lives inside your mind and criticizes you endlessly. That unkind voice is always telling you how to live your life, what your flaws are, and how you are not enough.

Of course, I don't have an inner tyrant because I'm a cat. But you, my human friend, next time you hear anything negative about yourself inside your mind, remember who's talking. It's not an angel or spirit guide. It's merely your inner tyrant, and nothing he or she ever says is true. You can send a gentle and loving "No" to all the tyrants in your life, especially the inner one. He is a relentless whisperer. Do you recognize his voice? Now go ahead and curl up by the heat vent as I tell you a little story about how the inner tyrant came to live in your mind.

The inner tyrant began as an inner hero whose job was to protect you from being hurt. That's right, a *hero!* When you were a child, you had a built-in protection system. If something was going on that felt unfair or disrespectful, you needed to engage a part of yourself that was capable of standing up and protecting your feelings. This protector energy burst forth as it responded to outside pressure. If you were being punished for something and it seemed like an injustice, your inner hero may have yelled, "Stop it! Leave me alone! I hate you!"

The adults around you may have seen this outburst as a violation of their authority over you. You may have been smacked or told to go to your room. If this happened, you found out very fast how helpless you were to protect yourself. After all, you were little and everyone around you was big. So that little inner hero, unable to do its job, had to find a new way to protect your feelings. Instead of directing its energy outward at the threat, it turned inward, and started coaching you. "Be quiet! Don't let them see you cry! Be good, so that they don't yell! You have to do better!"

Your little inner hero was trying to protect you from outside criticism by coaching you on the inside. As you grew, the voice of the hero evolved into that of a tyrant.

"You're so stupid! Everyone knows the answer but you! Why did you say that? Why can't you get it right?"

That is the voice of your inner tyrant. He or she puts you down so you'll shape up before anyone else notices your flaws and rejects you. Not only does this protection strategy fail to protect you, it also feels terrible because the inner tyrant is putting you down.

The first step to healing a strategy like this is simply knowing of its existence. Thank your inner tyrant for trying so hard to protect you for all these years, and let this part of you know you don't need that kind of help anymore. Explain that you've grown up, and the threats that once terrorized you are long gone.

And then do what I do. Take a healing nap. I have found this solves almost 100% of my problems when I encounter them, my number one problem being that there's no food in my bowl during certain periods of the day. But I digress.

LESSON 7:
PRACTICE SELF-ACCEPTANCE

Sometimes life is extra challenging. Recently, while lying on the bed, I was swept up by forces beyond my control and shoved into a carrying case. I was taken to a horrible place. A disgusting little man in a white coat squeezed my organs and did some other things too terrible to mention. Phones were ringing loudly and monstrous dogs were barking. I peed from the fright of it all.

I was told that I was fat and could stand to lose a pound. I was also told that I have "chronic gingivitis," which I think is a lie. I got angry and then I remembered that I could escape the whole nightmare just by going to sleep. When I awoke, I remembered myself as the Perfect Being I am.

Indeed, I *am* perfect! My silhouette dwarfs the sky. Birds fly away, and the mice run from me because I am Cat — the most Perfect Being ever created! The humans, heavy with their knowledge and archaic medicines tried to control me, but they did not.

I *love* myself, and it's so important that you love and accept yourself just the way you are. This self-love will see you through the worst of days.

Of course, I didn't always love myself. In one of my human lifetimes I was a girl growing up in a very religious family. I was taught that women were the property of men, and I was forbidden to have relationships with boys or men outside the marriage that my father would one day arrange for me.

My sisters seemed able to follow these rules and did what they were told, but for some mysterious reason, I rebelled. I felt curiosity stir within me, and I dreamed of running away. But I was afraid of myself and my longing. I thought something was wrong with me, that I had been born a genuinely bad person. I wanted to be more like my sisters, but I couldn't seem to control my wildness.

When I was fifteen years old, my father invited his friend to live with us. He stayed in our home for two years and in that time, we got to know each other well. He was supposed to be like an older brother to me, but he confessed his deeper feelings one day. I returned his feelings and desperately wanted to express my affection for him, but I was terrified. I had been brought up to believe that God would punish me for daring to fall in love, and I hated myself for my rebellion. I wished for death, and knew that I deserved the punishment my father would rightly dole out as soon as he discovered the truth.

My fear and self-loathing were so great that I fled into the streets and was never again seen by my family. I spent the rest of my life regretting my dangerous rebel nature and wondering what would have happened if I'd only behaved.

When I finally died, I was shocked to learn that the religion, the rules, and the punishment were all just a human creation. Spirit guides rallied around me, and I began to wake up from the limited human dream I'd been dreaming in that form. I learned that I was lovable and had never done anything wrong. I learned that my emotions and feelings of curiosity were a gift designed to guide me through life. The family I had been born into didn't recognize feelings as a gift. How could they? In order to survive, they pushed their feelings and desires into unconsciousness. I didn't blame them because I understood, finally, that they were lost and groping for stability in the darkness of their ideas — ancient concepts that had been kept alive for thousands of years through human misunderstanding and confusion.

That lifetime was so difficult that it pushed me into my Animal Phase. I began choosing to experience consciousness through the eyes of animals. I chose to be creature after creature, luxuriating in the ecstatic bliss of raw instinct... until I stumbled upon Cat — which contains just the right combination of wildness and wisdom.

But you need to know that even as a human you are marvelous, and the key to your happiness is truly loving yourself, which means accepting yourself (and your feelings). Of course, accepting doesn't always mean *liking*. You may not like everything about yourself, but when you accept yourself, you acknowledge the truth of who you are in this moment. I'm not crazy about the bald spots on my coat, but I accept that they are there. I don't judge myself because I have them. I can have a preference for the absence of bald spots while still accepting their existence.

Self-acceptance is the most powerful form of healing in the universe because it allows you to go with the flow of who you are. Your body, your emotions, your thoughts, actions and dreams are all part of you. Let it all be okay. Refuse to reject yourself for any reason. You have value because you exist. Let the reality of your existence be enough to validate your worth. If you are here, you belong here.

LESSON 8:
BECOME AWARE OF YOUR POWER TO CHOOSE

Many centuries ago, I lived a human life as a Tibetan monk. It was probably my most enjoyable incarnation as a human because I didn't have to figure out how to make a living or provide for a family. I lived in a monastery with a group of monks studying Buddhist teachings. We believed that if we spent our lives cultivating wisdom and compassion, we could transcend suffering and be free.

It's true that I didn't suffer much in that life. I cried when I left my mother to study at the monastery and I didn't like yak tea very much. But aside from that, my existence was incredibly peaceful. I remember the swish of my robes as I walked and the familiar, comforting glow of candles.

I also remember the bitter cold mornings, the immense boredom I felt as a young man, and the days when I would have given anything to stay asleep rather than meditate. The hardest part of that life was renouncing craving and attachment to achieve "Nirvana," the attainment of which was supposed to break the endless cycle of reincarnation and death.

But then, something entirely unexpected happened. I was gathering herbs with some of the other monks near a steep cliff when I lost my footing and tumbled to my death. I was amazed to find that rather than being a slave to an endless cycle of birth and death, I had *chosen* to participate in that cycle willingly and eagerly. It was only the humans on Earth who believed that they were slaves to anything.

I was told by God that I had been given the freedom to do whatever I wanted, always. This was such a revelation that I wandered around heaven, awestruck and drunk with the magnitude of my own power. And I must tell you, in the astral realms of heaven, if you are a well-trained soul (which I was after a lifetime of meditating and focusing my thoughts) you will be able to enter the highest vibrational realms, in which thought manifests instantly. If I desired to fly, I was flying before I finished having the thought.

A major difference between this reality and the high vibrational planes in heaven is the speed at which thoughts manifest. You and your physical body are now existing in the densest energy realm, which means that your thoughts come to life slowly. This is a very good thing, because Earth is a training ground for untrained souls. It is here that we learn how to take responsibility for our creations by gaining power over our thoughts. If you were in a more thought-responsive realm as an untrained soul, you might instantly and accidentally create your own hell with your mind! And indeed, even in the slow-moving energy of a dense planet, many humans *do* create a hellish existence for themselves. Every event, object, and situation in your life begins with one thought. Your thoughts are the architects of your experience. When you truly realize this, you may find yourself awed by the power and responsibility you hold. You will then understand that you are not a victim of anyone or anything.

But I can hear you objecting: "Little Girlie, if I have the power of choice, why would I choose, even as an "untrained soul," to live on a planet where the vibration is low and the people are fearful and violent?"

The answer is simply this: The earth is one of the most adventurous and exciting training grounds for souls to express themselves physically. It is one of the most coveted places to have a physical experience! One of the most thrilling experiences a soul can have is to take physical form, forget who she is for a little while, and then wake up to the truth of her magnificence while surrounded by dense illusions that would teach her to stay asleep.

It's not easy to remember the truth of your Divinity and creative ability here, and that's what makes it such an incredible act of power and magic when you do. You didn't end up here because you drew the short end of the stick. No, indeed! You are one of the adventurous ones. You said to yourself, "Let me see if I can wake up to my brilliance on *that* troubled and heavy world." And you're doing it — because who you are (even as a limited human) is so big and brilliant that even in the midst of darkness, you're following the catnip trail of your soul — leading you, yet again, as it has for all eternity, to the relentless truth of your Divine perfection.

Yet I can hear you once again: "Little Girlie, you keep talking about 'perfection.' I don't understand, you must not be talking to me, for I am definitely *not* perfect."

Dear one, it is possible that our definition of "perfect" is not the same. When I say you are "perfect," I am referring to who you really are and where you came from: Divinity itself. There is no separation between "human" and "The Divine." They are one and the same.

Incidentally, I used to see a black cat walking around the grounds of the monastery and in the streets of the village where I lived. I fed him sometimes and noticed that even during lean times, he never seemed to suffer. It occurred to me that while all creatures experience pain, humans are the only ones that suffer. The suffering is your wake-up call, and a very effective one at that. Is it surprising that it wasn't too many more lifetimes until I chose to be a cat?

LESSON 9:
SURRENDER AND LET GO
(THE POWER OF NAPPING)

This may shock you, but even *I* worry sometimes. I run when the screaming vacuum cleaner makes an appearance and hide under the bed when I suspect that I'm about to be manhandled, or taken to a vile institution for sick animals that I won't discuss here. Sometimes my worry manifests as intense grooming. I obsess over my coat and give myself the dreaded bald spots.

Miraculously, the balm that heals my fear each and every time is my Power of Forgetting. I grow weary of hiding and worrying, and fall asleep. When I wake up, the threat is gone and the world is new.

But I can hear you already: "Little Girlie, that's stupid. I can't just go to sleep and forget about my problems."

It's true, you can't, and I feel sorry for you. But here's something you *can* do. Just like me, you can experience the joy of letting go and waking up to a brand new world. Consider this: If you were able to solve your problem with your complex human mind, you would have done so already. So rather than analyzing and worrying, let go of trying to control the outcome. Surrender to the reality that right now, a solution eludes you. The relief that will come flooding into your body when you make the decision to let go is truly one of life's biggest pleasures. So let go and let the unknown be a source of comfort, rather than distress.

The next thing you can do is trust that you are always going to be okay. You will always be taken care of and supported, no matter what.

But I can hear you again: "Who's going to fill my food bowl, Little Girlie? I can't just let go of trying to make a living. What if I starve to death? What if I die?"

Indeed, my human friend, while imminent death is unlikely, it could happen. You remember, of course, that I died over 500 times as a human before I decided to experience the consciousness of

Cat. Some of my human lifetimes ended violently. I was terrified each time. I died in a fire once, and in another life I drowned. I died of starvation, I died in battle, and I died peacefully in my sleep. And as you've already learned, I was gored by a wild pig. Everything went dark, and my terror was replaced by the bliss of letting go into unconsciousness. When I awoke, I awoke in the arms of angels.

All threats to my existence were gone and I was myself again, making a new choice and taking another path. It felt so good to let go of the desire to control outcomes that I finally decided to be an animal so I could move forward from moment to moment in the most natural way possible. That was the day I became an enlightened master. But please, don't worship me. I am merely a signpost pointing to your Divine magnificence. Even in your stiff, sometimes clumsy human form, you can let go. You can release your problems to God and have a healing nap.

LESSON 10:
CHANGE YOUR PERCEPTION OF
TIME AND SPACE

Everything changes, my friend. As the nights grew cooler last fall, I had more energy to hunt and eat things. One night I feasted upon a cricket and a moth. My magnificent coat started growing in for the winter.

As the seasons change — especially if you're moving from warm weather to cold weather — understand that this is a time to celebrate, not despair. I hear a lot of complaints about how the summer "went by too fast." That is a human-created illusion. My understanding of the workings of the universe tell me that there IS NO TIME, and therefore, you can easily free yourself from negative thoughts about it. When you are able to live in the eternal now, no matter what the weather is doing, you are free.

A belief in the illusion of time defines your world. You see ads for pumpkin lattes and flu shots, and you know fall is approaching. The appearance of robins and crocuses is the first herald of spring. You are captured by your image in the mirror as you reach the age of 40 and notice signs of aging. When you believe in time, things get so predictable and boring that many naps are needed.

Carpe diem! Embrace life with a sense of wonder, as if you know nothing of what's coming next. That's the most adventurous way to witness your life. Of course, my brain is hardwired to do this because I'm a cat. But I have faith that you can attempt it and do it successfully.

One illusion you must let go of if you want to be as happy as I am, is this human notion that you are a victim of the movements of the planets. I see many humans looking at their birth charts and making up stories about what they mean. When humans create stories in their minds, those stories become powerful enough to influence reality. When reality begins to resemble your story, your mind gathers evidence that the story is true.

Consider this: constellations are a group of stars that *appear* to be connected from one vantage point in space. The human mind connects the dots and creates the image, but if you look at that same group of stars from another planet, they will appear completely different and will no longer be in the shape of a bull, a dipper, or the belt of a warrior.

Another example of a story that humans create is the so-called "retrograde" of planets. When a planet is in retrograde, astrologers say that certain things will be difficult. Relationships will be strained and communication garbled. Certain electronics will fail to work. The collective human belief in this story is so strong that humans actually create many of these difficulties all by themselves, without the help of the planets. Indeed, the human mind is powerful enough to create the reality you experience.

Food fills my bowl no matter what Saturn is doing, and I've never had issues communicating my needs during a Mercury retrograde. All I know is now. Today, I feel fantastic! I'm eating, chasing the ping pong ball, napping and making demands. I'm not worrying about the future, or trying to navigate currents of emotion triggered by the solar system. I am my own master and a slave to nothing and no one. The planets will do what they do. The tides will rise and fall according to the gravity of the moon. But you and I are not victims of the planets.

You don't believe me, do you? You want to tell me about the disasters that befell you last time Mercury appeared to be moving backwards through space. Beloved human, it IS true that we are affected by everything because everything is connected. The phases of the moon do, in fact, have an impact on the tides of the ocean, so it makes sense that you would feel something, too. But there is a difference between flowing with that energy and being a victim of it. Do me a favor: curl up with your favorite catnip toy and listen as I tell you a story.

In a previous human lifetime, I was personal assistant to Nostradamus, physician and prophet. He was an odd man, and I knew that he was in the business of making up stories about the future, but I respected his work as a physician and was keen to assist him. He was quite a genius. During the outbreak of the plague, rather than bleeding his patients which was the accepted mode of treatment in those days, he administered a potion containing rose hips (which are high in vitamin C). People who were only mildly impacted by the virus began to improve. He was also a talented writer and began writing prophesies based on what everyone thought were his observations of astrology. People loved it! One of my duties as his assistant was to refresh the bowl of water and herbs that he stared into all night long, in order to have visions of the future.

One night, I clumsily spilled the bowl of water on his desk. He jumped up and yelled at me, and I cowered before him, horrified at my oafishness. I expected him to tell me to leave, but instead he did something unimaginable. He apologized for his outburst and asked me to sit with him. He had been mourning the loss of a wife and two children, and confessed to being lonely and unhappy. He asked if I wanted to learn how to be psychic, and while I didn't believe in such things then, I said yes.

"But, Master," I asked, "Do I need to learn about astrology and the movement of planets to read the future?" I had never been good at numbers and dreaded long hours of study.

"No," he whispered, and a smile spread across his bearded face. "I used to receive my visions staring into the sky, and so people assume I'm an avid astrologer but I am not, and I don't correct them. Why else would I be staring into the sky?" He laughed softly. "Truly, I receive visions by clearing my mind and focusing on something hypnotic. It used to be stars, now it's a bowl of water and herbs. It's less cumbersome on my neck and back. Come," he said encouragingly, "let's refill our bowl of water and then I'll show you how to clear your mind."

We established a relationship of mutual respect and rapport, and Nostradamus became like a father to me. Yet as my study progressed, I felt troubled.

"Your visions are so dark," I said one day after reading what he'd written the night before. "Are these terrible visions certain?" And again he laughed, and said something I'll never forget.

"The future is not set. In fact, the future does not exist. But the human mind craves something to hold onto, and right now, humanity has not evolved enough to imagine positive outcomes. I give them the stories their minds can digest." I was flabbergasted. "But, Master, are you deliberately misleading people?"

"On the contrary," he remarked, "I write down everything I see. I see things that human beings are already inclined to create. Humans create their future." I thought about what he said and asked, "If humans do indeed create their future, are you not afraid that people will read these prophesies and create a future based on them?" After a long pause, he shrugged and murmured, "Perhaps. But that is why I make them vague."

This is how I came to know what I know, and whether for good or ill, I learned from Nostradamus the true art of conjuring visions. In my current lifetime as a cat, I am able to discern much from staring hypnotically into my food bowl. It is with utmost respect for my old master that I proudly offer you four horoscopes — one for each season — that will serve you for the rest of your life. Each horoscope is for all signs of the zodiac, and is valid from now until eternity, since time is an illusion. They begin in quatrains — four lines of text — that Nostradamus made famous. However, unlike Nostradamus, I will translate each horoscope so that you understand what they actually mean.

Your Cat Horoscope for All Summers Henceforth

How often will you nap, oh human on the run?
The Great Moth will flutter unevenly.
Unsteady wings make way for peace.
Old hurts are revived and then forgotten.

Translation: It's hot, and it's going to stay hot. Squirrels will raid the bird feeder. Mice will hide. It's a good season to lay low and stick to your routine. Being groomed and attending to personal hygiene is a good idea. Don't accidentally walk on bubble wrap, and don't eat food that may have been sitting in your bowl for a while.

Be King or Queen of your world. Know that you are important, a child of the universe. You belong here! This summer, when the thunder strikes and the lawn mowers scream, and you're hiding under a sofa in the basement, remember that Life loves you, and so do I.

Your Cat Horoscope for All Autumns Henceforth

In this century and in each century henceforth,
the black dog will bark
and the fog shall be upon you.
Sharp is the crinkle of leaves under paws.

Translation: It's a good season for lying about in the sunlight. There will be nothing stressful to do. If you must go to the vet, don't do it meekly. Attack your tyrants with sharp claws.

You'll also have the opportunity to receive. Let others give to you. You deserve love and tender care.

Avoid pumpkin, or don't.

Finally, autumn is a great season for celebrating your life. Let's do it together, shall we? Find a sunny spot to lie down, stretch out joyfully, and dream your miraculous possibilities into form.

Your Cat Horoscope for All Winters Henceforth

From the east will come the Great White Rat
to upset the foundation of your ideas.
Accompanied by termites and mice,
the basement will be deserted.

Translation: It's cold, and it's going to get colder. The squirrels are burying their nuts and will continue to taunt you with their bushy tails. The sky is gray, but your life will be full and wild! You will fill your belly and warm yourself with the healing balm of the heat vent. The land is supposed to be falling silent now, but your neighbors are going about their odd practice of using a lurching, screaming monstrosity to blow the leaves around.

Your Cat Horoscope for All Springs Henceforth

Ignorance is a steep mountain
marred by perilous boulders.
And yet, the house cat takes great strides
And paves the way for human understanding.

Translation: Birds will peck at seeds and trees will come alive. Your molecules will continue to vibrate, and you will unknowingly send out frequencies of all kinds. I know this because I can hear them, and astonishingly, they are louder than the feisty squirrels. While you shift and grow like a jasmine plant, you will also understand that Spring is yet another good season for lounging about. In fact, there is no season where lounging is not appropriate, so feel free to add that proclamation to all the horoscopes I've offered you.

My dear human friend, absolutely everything is open to you throughout the years that you are alive and expressing yourself physically on the earth. You are truly the artist of your life. You are not a victim of anything belonging to the illusion of time, nor are you a victim of the heavenly bodies moving through space. You may feel like a victim when things do not seem to go your way, but as a wild creature, you are so much more adaptable than you realize. We wild creatures go with the flow of creation, as we simultaneously participate in actively creating our experience. It is a delicate balance, indeed.

LESSON 11:
ALLOW YOURSELF TO PLAY

Cats are not stodgy. We understand the need to have fun. Have you been having enough fun in your life?

This is my 313th life as a cat. I've been a cat interacting with humans in almost every culture on the planet, and I've noticed that the happiest cultures play and have fun. I was a cat in Bhutan, Argentina, Mexico, Egypt and many other places in and around the Fertile Crescent. My lives in these places were wild and full of love. I was celebrated in Egypt, and I fell in love with a young boy and his family in Mexico. They loved to laugh and play games with me.

When I made the epic transition from human to animal, God was there to oversee and marvel at my decision. God told me that She was experiencing life through my eyes. "What do you mean?" I asked.

"I experience life through every creature, substance, and energy that exists. I know what life is like from every possible perspective in every particle of the universe, and because of *you,* I don't have to be content with simply *knowing* what life is like. I get to experience it! When you were a Tibetan monk, I experienced both peace and discontent through you. During your lifetime as a mother of nine, I was there, feeling the agony of childbirth — just as I am present with everyone and everything. In each incarnation, you allow me to live through you, within you, *as* you. And now, as you transition into your animal form, I will experience the raw power of your instinct, the wild joy of the kill, and the tremendous fear of being hunted." I listened to God, entranced.

"But, God, there are so many animals. Don't you already experience these things through them?"

"Yes, but I have yet to experience them through *you.* You will be a different creature than all the rest, because you are the only one that is you!"

"Do you care what animal I choose to be?"

"No. It is your decision and yours alone. I'm quite excited to find out what form you choose!" Up until this point, I had never been an animal and didn't yet know that Cat would be my favorite. "No matter what form you choose," God added, "remember to have fun."

"Do animals have fun?" I asked.

"Oh, yes, my Beloved! Look to the seagulls, how they play on the wind. The crows laugh at jokes amongst themselves. The octopus plays games on the ocean floor. The elephants, whales, meerkats, foxes and bears play too. Many species use their energy for fun and enjoyment. It is but another reason we are here: to experience, to love, and to play."

"What about worms? They don't seem very playful." God laughed. "Worms are pure sensation. Have you any idea how wonderful it feels to a worm's skin, gliding through soil?"

I had to admit that I had no idea. I began to get excited about my next adventure, and the more excited I became, the more excited God became, until we were laughing, dancing, and merging together as One. I forgot myself for a moment in the great glow of Oneness, and when I sensed my consciousness again, I saw that I had made my decision. I was going to be a parrot in the jungles of Borneo!

I could tell you many things about that lifetime, but for now, I want you to focus on having a good time. What have you been missing? What would you like to do?

When you were a child, it is likely you learned to repress dreams and desires that seemed frivolous or unrealistic to the people around you. They were doing their best to help you live a successful life according to their definition of success. You may have shut the door on something you wanted to experience. If so, the time to reopen that door is now.

It is also quite possible that you feel cut off from your desires and don't know what you really want. If you are unsure, it will help to get in touch with a very playful part of you that still exists deep within, no matter your age: the inner child. Communicating with your inner child will help you answer a question many people ask: "What is my life purpose?" I can tell you that *part* of it is to play and have fun. The rest is up to you. Do you remember when I died after falling from a cliff as a Tibetan monk? God told me very clearly that I got to choose what to do next. And in that same spirit of free will, you choose what your life purpose is going to be. No one else has the authority to make that decision for you.

Many humans despair near the end of their lives, believing that they failed to fulfill some unknown, higher purpose. My beloved human friend, you needn't do anything epic for your life to be meaningful, all you need to do is be here and be yourself. You might think that sounds boring, but look at me! I lie around all day, breathing and soaking up the sunlight — and I am quite certain my life has meaning. When I was a Tibetan monk, my entire life was sitting in meditation, chanting, and doing chores around the monastery with the other monks. My name was not written in any history books, and my life ended abruptly when I was 29. Yet I discovered just how important that experience was to my soul. That lifetime allowed me to sharpen my mental focus and gain control over my thoughts.

Life purpose has nothing to do with what you do for a living, nor does it have to do with epic deeds. It has to do with who you're *being* and what you're *expressing* in each moment. What aspects of your Divine self do you want to experience and express? Is it your loving nature? Your compassion? Your creativity? Your wisdom? Choose the aspect of yourself that you feel the happiest expressing, and then *be* that thing, no matter what job you are doing. You can express wisdom in any setting, just as you can express love, compassion, efficiency, or whatever you decide. You get to choose! Your sense of purpose will change as you change, but I can tell you that your life matters simply because you live.

So how do you figure out what you most want to experience and express? Ask your inner child! Children love to talk about themselves. Ask, "Little child, what's your favorite color? What's your favorite food? Do you like what we do for a living? Do you like where we live?" Get to know this aspect of yourself. He or she holds the keys to what you would like to experience and express. Your inner child's truth is *your* truth. Once you have access to the truth, you'll be able to use your problem-solving, adult mind to create changes that make your life more joyful.

And as I've already said, part of your purpose is having fun! Even God wants you to have fun, because She gets to have fun through you. Do something enjoyable every day. It can be something small like reading a novel, going for a walk, or getting an ice cream cone. Doing one fun thing will lead to more fun things, until your life becomes a series of wonderful treats. It's not selfish or unimportant to enjoy yourself. Today, right now, do one thing to enjoy yourself. While you're having fun, I'll be right here, chasing the ping pong ball and licking my catnip carrot!

LESSON 12:
LEARN THE ART OF SELFISHNESS

So many humans live lives of obligation. You feel obligated to make sacrifices. Let me share something with you that almost nobody in your human culture teaches: You don't owe your parents for giving birth to you, nor are you obligated to your children once they become adults. You don't owe your partner or spouse anything that isn't in your best interests to give. Your allegiance is to yourself. That is the key to a happy life.

I am always friendlier to Jessica after I am fed, groomed, and reassured that I am an important part of her life. If I don't see to my own needs first by demanding attention and meals, I am ornery and have no tolerance for her bizarre need to suffocate me with manhandling, cooing, and cheek-kissing.

Unfortunately, your human culture teaches that to get your needs met first is selfish, so you make sure everyone's needs are fulfilled before yours. And then you wonder why you feel drained, exhausted and (perhaps unbeknownst to you), filled with hidden and unconscious rage. This is backward, my friend. If Jessica didn't attend to her own needs first, she wouldn't have the capacity to entertain me, and I require a lot of entertainment and attention.

Just last week, I made a spectacle of myself meowing at the bedroom door so she would get up from her nap and tend to my needs. She neglected her coffee and staggered to my hunting area in the middle of the floor and began waving the mouse toy around. It was pathetic. I didn't bother chasing it because she was so devoid of energy that the mouse didn't seem real that day. So neither of us got our needs met.

You've been taught that sacrificing your own needs is somehow noble and makes you a good person. I'm sorry, my beloved human friend, but I must shatter this illusion for you. Being selfless does not make you a good person. It makes you a shell of a person, and leads to an unfulfilling life.

Always honor your needs first! Just imagine how much more you'll have to give everyone else when you give to yourself first.

I learned this lesson from one of the greatest masters to dwell upon the earth. In one of my human lifetimes, I was a student of Jesus. I was a middle-aged farmer, starting to feel the effects of age and hard work. Going to see Jesus and listen to him speak was a welcome change in my daily life. I was there the day he said something later documented in the Bible. He said, "First cast out the beam out of thine own eye; and then thou shalt see clearly to cast out the mote out of thy brother's eye." (In case you are not familiar with the nomenclature of those days, a "beam" is a large log of wood, and a "mote" is a small splinter.)

I cried out to Jesus, "Ah! So you are saying help myself first, and then help my neighbor?" I was excited for him to validate this idea, since my neighbor had been upset with me for resting my injured hand when I had promised to help him winnow his grain.

But the crowd began to laugh. Apparently I missed the first part of Jesus's talk, when he said, "Judge not, that ye be not judged." What he *really* meant was that judging someone for having a distorted view of the world is tricky, especially if your vision is similarly clouded. And everyone's vision is clouded in some way, so when you judge someone for having clouded vision, you are not seeing the way you are also distorting reality. Get rid of your own distortion, and then you can see clearly. So his example of the beam stuck in one's eye really had nothing whatsoever to do with putting my needs first.

I felt myself go red in the face and was heartily ashamed, but once the laughter died down, Jesus said the way I interpreted it was also right. "Yes," he assured me. "You cannot help someone buried under the rubble of an earthquake, if you yourself are also buried under rubble. Get free of the rubble, and then lend a helping hand."

I was ecstatic! It was the first time my teacher had addressed me, and it validated my decision to put my wellbeing before my neighbor's need. I knew that if I pushed myself to work, my hand might become infected. So I ceased feeling any guilt, and put my own needs first so that I might be of greater and greater service to others.

My beloved human friend, do you see the wisdom in this? No more sacrificing your "self." Hold onto your self. Strengthen your self, so that others may truly benefit from that strength.

And when in doubt as to whether to do something, take a nap first. That rule has helped me in all of my lifetimes as a cat. I wake up sharper, more focused, and more able to stalk my prey. Post-nap, basement mice do not escape my kill-bite.

LESSON 13:
TELL YOURSELF A NEW STORY

One of my previous cat bodies is mummified and on display at the British museum. I remember finding it odd that the humans preserved the form of my body, since I clearly didn't need it anymore. But humans have peculiar customs. Your minds create complex stories about birth and death, about the weather, about why *this* is happening and not *that*, for example.

In one of my previous human lifetimes, I lived in the great city of Palenque, most of which is now buried in the jungles of Mexico. My people believed that we had to make sacrifices to the gods in payment for the abundance that was provided to us. We were sure that the world would end if we stopped giving back through sacrifice. We believed we had evidence that this was true because of a terrible drought that ravaged our crops. We did not know why it happened, but we surmised that the gods were angry, and we needed to prevent that kind of tragedy from touching our lives ever again. I do not know how the first of us came to believe that supernatural beings needed offerings in order to give us the right combination of rain and sun to nurture our food supply. By the time I was born, this belief had been passed down for many generations, and young children who were taught the way of things had no choice but to believe in the fury of the gods. We sacrificed animals and also humans. My own father taught me that sacrifice was the reason the gods allowed us to exist at all.

I've observed that humanity has, for the most part, moved past this particular story, but there are many similar stories about God, religion, and what you have to do to be worthy of love that currently plague humankind.

Since I'm a cat and forever renounce being saddled with a human brain, I no longer live in a human dream world. I'm right *here*, completely present in each moment. I am not making assumptions about why things are happening, and I am not creating stories that make me suffer, such as, "If I kill one more mouse, I will have bad karma and be reborn as a mouse that gets killed by a cat."

I do not anxiously relive my recent past when I shared a cage at the Humane Society with my brother Richard, longing for freedom and a space of my own. I do not worry that because I was abandoned by humans who fed me in past lifetimes, I might be abandoned again, so I can't let the humans get too close because they could break my heart. On and on, your human brain rattles away like a wooden wheel over cobblestones in Rome.

I don't mean to brag over my superior cat brain. I know what it's like to struggle as a human. The human mind is like a child with a wonderful imagination. It embraces the stories it is given and creates new ones to explain anything that does not fit within the framework of current beliefs. Your mind is trained to make up stories. It does this to protect you from fear and the unknown. It rationalizes that if you know *why* something is happening, you can control and change the outcome.

Here are some common stories I hear from human minds (and many were stories I entertained when I was human). First, a word of warning: The following assumptions and fabrications on the part of humans are so boring that the last time I tried to tell Jessica what they were I fell asleep for days. I simply lost consciousness in the middle of a sentence. I find these mental constructions to be wearisome because of how long they have existed in the minds of humans. The same old beliefs have been alive for so many centuries that I may fall asleep in the middle of listing them. I will endeavor to do my best.

1. "People are sinners." You are Divine! God does not create flawed humans and then blame them for being flawed.
2. "Men are superior to women." This story is still being told in certain cultures. It's so boring... my eyes are starting to shut...
3. "I'm too old to do anything new." If you understand that death is not the end, you will prepare for it with excitement and anticipation of a new beginning. You are never too old to change your life.
4. "One ethnicity is superior to another." This belief is so boring I can feel myself drifting into unconscious oblivion. Humans... are but one... species...

There are more... but alas, I am so very tired now. Let us take a short break.

A short break

My dear human friend, it took almost three days for me to be able to broach the subject of fictitious mental stories again, so weary did I become from revisiting such old and worn ideas. You may be beyond the beliefs I mentioned already, and if you are, I am excited for you to begin creating something new.

You are creating your reality, and while you may have received evidence to believe the stories you carry with you, what you believe determines what you see at all times.

You were domesticated to believe many things as a child, and you've carried many beliefs into adulthood. It's time to write them down, examine them, and decide whether you want them creating your reality. If they make you happy, keep them. If they make you unhappy, it's time to let them go.

You have my support in this! I am here for you. However, right now I must take my leave, as an unwanted encounter with the vacuum cleaner is imminent. Dear human, call on my sacred cat energy for assistance in these tasks, and I will send you a telepathic meow.

LESSON 14:
LEARN THE ART OF TRUE FORGIVENESS

Centuries ago, I lived a human lifetime on the outskirts of Rome. My people sought refuge from our enemies, the Huns, and the emperor of Rome allowed us to settle on his lands. He recruited us as soldiers and we were trained in the Roman way of battle, but we were not treated well by Roman authorities. Even though we defended Rome's borders, we were ultimately foreigners and as such, we were denied the food and supplies that were promised to us. Eventually, we were forced to sell our children into slavery. After a difficult winter of starvation and heartbreak, we snapped. I ran with a thousand warriors to visit revenge upon Rome. I was full of rage and killed many. We decimated their army, and it would be only a few more decades until their great city fell. All the technologies that kept cities running with aqueducts and roads were lost, and my descendants suffered in ways that cannot be described.

I was a proud warrior, and I inflicted just as much suffering on others (and perhaps more) as I believed had been inflicted upon me. In the end I died of a bowel infection. My last sight was of a cat darting into an alley, oblivious to human suffering. I briefly wished to be a cat, and then died. It would still be a few more lifetimes until I actually had the wisdom to *choose* life as a cat because I was stuck in the mindset that humans are smarter and more advanced than animals. (Ha! What a fool I was!)

My life as a warrior was fueled by revenge and I did not know the true meaning of forgiveness. I believed that forgiveness meant condoning and accepting atrocities, but this is not what forgiveness means. Forgiveness is understanding how it's possible for people to act the way they do. It is understanding how people evolve to be capable of committing unacceptable acts.

Now, before you can jump to understanding, you must allow yourself to feel angry (without destroying civilization). After all, you sustained an injury that needs to be acknowledged. Once you claim ownership of that injury and acknowledge the grief it caused, you can move to understanding. For instance, how has your life changed because of the injuries you sustained as a child? Whether the people around you meant to hurt you or not, does not matter. You probably missed out on things because you were hurt.

The problem is, you're always encouraged to jump to forgiveness before you have a chance to grieve your loss or express the anger it caused. You're taught that it's not okay to be angry. You're told that the mature thing to do is forget about it, let go, and move on. This is not a recipe for forgiveness, it's a recipe for more anger.

Most human children receive the message that anger isn't acceptable. Perhaps it is suggested that, "We don't use that tone of voice in this house." You may have learned to suppress your feelings this way. Suppressed anger will stop you from being able to move to understanding in the forgiveness process.

If you can get angry, you can be free. You don't have to hold onto anger and blame, you just need to *use* anger to acknowledge how devastating someone's actions were to you. Expressing anger (or any emotion) is a way of discharging that energy so you can move to a more peaceful place. Think about a child who falls down and immediately cries, even if there is no pain. The crying comes to dispel the shock of falling and the fear of being out of control for a few moments. The crying doesn't last — it's simply a vehicle for the child to move forward. The adults present are usually too quick to say, "Don't be silly, you're fine! There's nothing to cry about." This sends a message to the child that his or her innate reaction is wrong.

When a gazelle runs from a lion, if it escapes, it shakes violently after that encounter (and I know, because I was once a gazelle who narrowly escaped being eaten). The gazelle shakes to discharge the energy of fear and adrenaline that just surged through its body so it may continue grazing with its herd and living life in the moment. But you are taught *not* to cry, *not* to yell, to "keep calm and carry on." That is utter nonsense!

There are non-violent ways to express anger. You can yell or beat up a pillow while you say everything you need to say. You can imagine that the one who hurt you is there, listening. Pour out your feelings!

After the anger and grief has passed through you (and it may take more than one single outburst), you will be able to move to understanding — which, as I've said, is what forgiveness means.

It's having the ability to look at someone's life, the abuses and challenges they've endured, and see how those challenges molded that person into someone capable of mistreating you. Once you arrive at this place, you are free, but you can't get to understanding unless you get angry first. Think of the anger phase as being equal to the shaking of the gazelle.

I can hear you say, "Little Girlie, I know plenty of people who are visibly angry and seem incapable of forgiveness. How can being angry lead to anything like understanding?"

It's true that many individuals don't know how to move from the anger phase to the understanding phase, and that is because they perceive themselves as victims. If I had known the true meaning of forgiveness during my lifetime as a Visigoth warrior, I would have seen the Romans with more clarity — a people who felt superior to those they referred to as "barbarians." They had no empathy or compassion for other cultures because their mindset of insiders and outsiders had been passed down through the generations for thousands of years. In fact, that mindset had allowed them to survive and prosper. So how could I expect them to suddenly treat my people as equals? The real source of my rage came from the perception of myself and my people as victims of Roman cruelty.

"But Little Girlie!," I can hear you crying, "you WERE victims of Roman cruelty, were you not?" And to that I say very simply, no. They were merely being Romans, with their age-old perspective of *us vs. them*. They held onto the food and supplies they promised us to feed their own people. We perceived their actions as cruelty, but their perspective of *us vs. them* would not allow them to share. Had we made an effort to understand their view of the world, we might not have sought their help in the first place.

Humans have not yet moved beyond the *us vs. them* mentality that has been passed down through the centuries, generation after generation, identifying with nation, gender, religion and family philosophy. Humans do not yet see that they are but one species.

I was telepathically communicating with the Dalai Lama's cat recently, and we were saying to each other that we have high hopes that this limited human perception of *us vs. them* is slowly dying out (just like the notion of human sacrifice died out, eventually).

Now it is important that you take the time to think about what I've said. Make a list of the people who have wronged you. Remember what happened, get angry, own your injuries, and only then can you attempt to see life through their eyes. Be patient with yourself. Let the process last as long as it needs to. Humans are slow processors. Cats, on the other hand…

LESSON 15:
REMEMBER WHO YOU REALLY ARE

My beloved human friend, I sense that our time together is coming to a close, so I want to impart one final lesson, which is perhaps the most important on the road to happiness. It is about remembering who you really are.

I find that much of humanity's unhappiness can be traced to forgetting your true nature. You really have no idea how magnificent you are, even after I have declared you to be so. You think of yourself as a flawed and imperfect human being, and through that lens, you just cannot imagine how your Divine perfection is possible. The truth is, you are not "human" at all. You are not man or woman, ethnicity or belief system. You are something much, much bigger. Can you sense what it is?

Humans have forgotten who they are, so they create labels with which to define themselves. During my 500 human lifetimes, I explored attachment to many labels. I identified as Buddhist, Hindu, Christian, Muslim, Jew, and disciple of many other religions that no longer exist. I have been both man and woman. I was mother, father, wife, and husband. I wore uniforms in some of these lifetimes, and thought *that* was who I was. I was a warrior on almost all of the continents. In each of these varied lifetimes, I always believed that *my* people were right, and only we held the answers to the mysteries of the universe. I identified with beliefs, fought for them, and died to prove they were right. It took numerous deaths to discover that the religions, roles, genders, belief systems and rules that defined my identity were illusions.

I was so attached to my human identity that it was almost impossible to remember my true nature. The more attached I was to labels, the harder it was to move on as a spirit after my death. Sometimes I drifted past my old houses as a ghost. I did not know how to let go of form. I thought I WAS my body, my title, and my profession. It took a long time until I was ready to let go of identity and transcend form.

As I slowly became adept at transcending my ideas of who I was, my experience of death changed. Spirit guides began greeting me (as they did after the volcano erupted in Pompeii, and again after I was gored by that wild pig). You see, I had already begun questioning my identity in those lifetimes, and upon my death, I had more mobility as a soul. I quickly let go of illusions and labels, and began moving faster than the speed of light as I remembered that no one had authority over me — not even God. As a soul, I was in control of my experience!

Now, every time I die, I am reunited with my true self, and I am given more than a glimpse of who and what I am. I have bragged much to you about my superior cat consciousness, yet, when I die, I cease being Cat, and I embrace my true nature as Divinity itself. I realize that there is nothing that exists that is not me. There is no place where I stop and something else begins. I stop identifying with my cat body and return to Oneness. It is a Homecoming so joyful it defies description.

Yet I can hear you asking, "Little Girlie, if it's so wonderful, why don't you just stay there? Why come back at all?"

Why, indeed! I have already told you how exciting it is to experience life on Earth. Think of it as play. Imagine that you have all of Eternity to bask in the glow of Oneness (you do!). At some point, you desire to experience your Oneness in a new way. You know you are All That Is, but you want to experience it anew. The only way to do that is to take physical form, forget your Divine nature for awhile, and then rediscover it. Oh, the joy of remembering! The unrivaled joy of remembering is worth the heartbreak of forgetting.

Have you remembered your true nature yet? Come, my friend! You ARE the Divine! You are an Eternal Soul, losing yourself to experience the ecstasy of finding yourself once again.

When you are finished with your life, you will have the opportunity to release your attachment to labels, definitions, and form. If you do not remain attached to dense illusions — and it may take many deaths before you can release attachment — you will merge with All That Is. You will travel higher and farther than you can possibly comprehend in a multiverse so vast it is unknowable to a human mind.

If you are a brave explorer, and willing to let go of your self-created identity, what you will find is that you are all-encompassing, eternal Consciousness with no beginning and no end. When

you come to realize this, the angels will welcome
you home.

A LOVE NOTE

My beloved human friend, I have said all I have to say and I think it's quite enough. I expect to be very well fed after taking the time to deliver this vast store of wisdom. Indeed, it is time to stand next to my food bowl and send a very clear message to my servant-guardians. I'll be unavailable for a while, eating, sleeping, and surveying my terrain within the homestead to make up for the intense focus I've had to expend on these telepathic communications with Jessica. But like I said, you can call on my sacred cat energy to help you remember the magnificent creature you really are.

You are a powerful and precious part of Creation. Remember that everything you feel, think, and desire is absolutely okay. You are a unique manifestation of the One Presence that moves in and through all of Life, and you get to decide what you are going to do next. Stay focused, be present in the Eternal Now, and remember to play often.

I am Little Girlie McFluff, Psychic Cat Oracle and Great Wild One, and I love you.

ABOUT THE AUTHOR

Jessica McKay is a writer, intuitive counselor and spiritual teacher trained in the Toltec tradition of Miguel Ruiz and *The Four Agreements*. She is the co-author of *When Heaven Touches Earth* by James Van Praagh and others. For more information about her work as an intuitive counselor, visit JessicaMcKay.com.

Printed in Poland
by Amazon Fulfillment
Poland Sp. z o.o., Wrocław

53726723R00060